I0788672

This Book Belongs To:

____

BY
Home Planners And
Journals
To help you organize your life

This book is copyright protected.
Reproducing this book is prohibited
and not allowed without the
permission of the author. All rights
reserved.

www.ingramcontent.com/pod-product-compliance
Lightning Source LLC
Chambersburg PA
CBHW071219240726
48654CB00009B/845